What are you going to do when they come for you?

Delores A. Allen

authorHOUSE®

AuthorHouse™
1663 Liberty Drive
Bloomington, IN 47403
www.authorhouse.com
Phone: 1-800-839-8640

First published by AuthorHouse   01/27/2012

ISBN: 978-1-4685-3727-7 (sc)
ISBN: 978-1-4685-3728-4 (ebk)

Library of Congress Control Number: 2011963736

Printed in the United States of America

Any people depicted in stock imagery provided by Thinkstock are models, and such images are being used for illustrative purposes only.
Certain stock imagery © Thinkstock.

This book is printed on acid-free paper.

Author has authorization for using Dake's Notes for her quotations.

TABLE OF CONTENTS

H onoring every Pastor that God has appointed to impart, exemplify and speak life to my inner man I do Love each of them to Life with a Godly and Sincere Love. My prayer is that God continue to bless and keep each one of them.

Present to pass

Apostle Marvin L. Smith taught me how to put my Faith in Action by allowing the word of God to be apart of me as I experienced a fathers love through all of your rebukes and corrections as you have taught me that my mind is blessed, because I am the just of God.

Pastor A Ray Rouson, taught me to walk in the knowledge of the Word of God, that I may receive wisdom from God, and how to love people with the love of God.

The late Pastor Cristina Rouson taught me how to stand bold in the face of adversity and disappointments as I bass in the presence of God and to enter into the experience of His SHEKINAH Glory.

Pastor Gregory Chapman—My spiritual brother who exemplified endurance and strength in the face of adversity and persecution while standing, and not being moved through the word of God.

Pastor Al-Jones exemplified loving me to life while allowing the anointing of God to unveil and give awesome Revelations in my life.

To The late Pastor Heart for baptizing me at the age of nine (9) exemplifying to me that I was safe in the arms of God. May you rest in peace Pastor Heart.

SPECIAL DEDICATION

————•❈•————

To; Elder Darlene Wallace
Who has been a pure delight and blessing as she has encouraged me
while I was in process of writing this book
May God continue to prosper you in every area of your life.

To; Pastor Ricky and Darlene Tolliver
For your encouraging prayers and teachings in the word of God

PREFACE

---·•❋•·---

What are you going to do when they come for you is a question that should be asked of every human being as they journey in this life time, because the majority of the human race will experience the introduction of oppression and depression. Some people will experience being in this state longer than others.

This question may derive from the unpleasant experiences and events in their past and present life. They may be introduced to oppression and depression through their genealogy lineage as well. These experiences will invade the seat of the mind set, and ultimately causing chemicals in the brain to become unbalance and dysfunctional. Not in the way that God has designed them to function.

This may cause the individual to function or act in an unhealthy state which affects every fiber of their being. This is a subject that needs to be addressed in the church as well as the medical institutions. It is a fact of life to every human being regardless of ethnic, age, status, gender, religion, nationality, weather rich or poor it has no respect for persons.

What are you going to do when they come for you is a question that gives the reader revelation through teachings and testimonies as well as hope, and insight to motivate and empower every individual as they seek answers that they have been seeking through the word of God.

This book conveys the Bio of Minister Delores A. Allen. And it is paralleled with inspirational biblical messages and applications as well as some scientific knowledge to help the reader to be encouraged, inspired, healed, delivered and ultimately sat free in these areas of their life by the miraculous power of Jehovah God through Jesus Christ by faith.

THIS BOOK IS DEDICATED TO

Jehovah My God, who gave his only begotten son Jesus Christ and His Holy Spirit who have and still is guiding me through every experience in my life, I give God all of the glory. I love you Deity

Harvey T. Allen Jr., my wonderful husband who has stood by me through it all, showing me much love and supporting me in my ministry and in the writing of this book. I love you honey.

Kentarsha and Kenita Atkins, my two beautiful daughters who wittiness my life as I journey through every trial as they have encouraged and loved me through it all. Remember to always stay close and love each other. That this bond of love shall continue to journey through your children and your children's children. I love you girls.

Doris and Shirley Atkins, my two wonderful sisters, who have been there with me and who have loved me the way Momma has raised us to love each other, without ever judging me. Sisters I love you with all my heart.

My linage, of the future generations to come, May you be healed delivered and set free through the love, knowledge and wisdom of God now and forevermore.

I can remember waking up early on a winter morning, feeling wet; then discovering that my baby sister Shirley (Bay-Bay) had wet the bed. My sister Doris and I complained about the wetness as we cuddled close together to stay warm in that full size bed.

I don't know why Shirley didn't wake up and tell us that she had to go to the bathroom; I suppose it was too cold. But the pee bucket was on the floor at the foot of the bed so we wouldn't have to go upstairs to the bathroom.

It was a cold morning. I hear mama stirring around in the front room. I can hear her trying to put some coal in the pot belly stove so that we could all get warmed up before we got out of bed. Looking at both of my sisters was always kind of strange for me because they both looked like me, except Bay Bay had red sandy hair and dimples. She was so pretty and special to us because she was the baby girl. She was also mean to us most of the time.

Doris looked very much like me. We had black hair, and no dimples, that I could see. But it was like looking into a mirror. She sounded like me when she spoke. Mama said that we were twins; but we all looked like momma. Wow we all looked alike.

As mama got us up to take a bath, we were all in tears. It was so cold that morning. We stood around the pot belly stove to get warm. We stood on the cold wood floor. We knew that the rest of the house would get warm when the stove got red hot. And just before it got red hot, my baby sister Shirley said to me and Doris, "you don't believe I'll put my belly to the stove?" And we said to her "you better not do that." And just as sure as we could finish telling her not to do it, she did it. She screamed very loud, and burst out crying. This was a busy morning for mama. And I just couldn't believe that Shirley did this. But she did.

Well it wasn't enough for Shirley to be wet from wetting the bed, now she had a painful scar on her belly as well. She was hard headed.

I guess we weren't old enough to go to school yet, because after mama cleaned us up and put some clothes on us, we would look out of the upstairs window and watch the older kids walk to school. I couldn't wait to go to school. That was part of being a big girl and I wanted to grow up fast.

I'M A BIG GIRL NOW

It must have been a year later, because I could remember mama holding Doris and my hand as we walked to Diggs Park Elementary School. The school was located across from the neighborhood projects for low income housing families. The project's name was Diggs Park, which was under the Norfolk redevelopment housing authority. It was about three miles from our house on Joyce Street.

It was all so new to me. I can still smell my new crayons and also seeing my new blue hardback tablet, and fat pencils. I can't recall having a book bag at that time. They split me and Doris up in a different class because we were identical twins. The teachers and students kept getting us mixed up. I was glad because I got tired of people marveling at us like they had never seen twins before. I guess we were the first set of twins people ever saw. The attention was overwhelming and it got pretty old most of the time. People were always asking us if we were twins. And what were our names. Bay Bay waited with mama for us to come home from school and she made sure that our chores were done.

Everyone knew Doris and Delores. They called my baby sister Shirley, (Miss Ann) because she always acted like the oldest. She thought she was our mama too. She always took up for us in the neighborhood as well as school age. She didn't want anyone to bother her twin sisters. She would fight for us and she would also fight us as well. She was one year and six months younger than we were. She entered school shortly afterward,

MAMA'S 3 BIG GIRLS

Later on the three of us would walk to school together, and we enjoyed it. We always had much to talk about on the way to school. There was a school crossing guard by the name of Ms. Dorothy Mae. She made sure we crossed the street. Mama taught us our address on Joyce Street in the Campostella section of Norfolk Virginia. I couldn't believe it, the three of us were big girls now.

After school we would change our clothes, do our chores, and play jump rope in the middle of the street. We would also play hop scotch with no shoes on our feet in the summer time. The streets didn't have much asphalt on them as they do today; the streets were mostly bumpy and rocky. As children we also played cowboys and robbers. Many children in the neighborhood played with us. We didn't have electronic games to play with as we do today, but boy didn't we have fun. We even played house and would pretend that we were adults. We played a lot under the tree in the backyard. We loved climbing the tree too. Yet mama was always observant toward us. She was also overprotected of us around men and boys.

Mama loved us so much. She taught us that no matter what happened in our lives that we were to always love one another. And if anything ever happened to her before we were grown, that we should never be split up. Mama was so pretty. I loved to look at her. I can still remember how her skin would smell and her pretty black hair. I wanted to be so much like her. She was the nicest person you would ever want to meet. She would always give to people who were in need. Sometimes she would give our food to someone else if they seemed to be hungry, even though we didn't have much money or food for ourselves.

I believe we lived most of the time on love alone. There was so much love amongst Mama, Doris, Shirley and myself. Yet it was this love that made the world go around for me. Even though we didn't have much money, or anything else for that matter, our needs were met most of the time. And when the needs weren't met, we still somehow survived. Mama was the youngest sibling of nine children. Big mama, Alice Pittman, (her mother) was a hard working woman. She always seemed to make ends meet. She loved all of her grandchildren the same. I loved eating at big mama's house; the food was so, so good.

In 1965 I can remember mama getting into this savings club with the neighbors to save money for Christmas. It was one of the best Christmas that you could imagine. We all got ten speed bicycles that year along with dolls, games and clothes. This was the best Christmas we have ever had in our lives. We thought that we were dreaming. And to top it off, some months later, mama brought us a television, which showed black and white at that time. You had to put money into it to play. Sometimes we weren't able to watch a complete television show. What a let down. Yet we were still grateful to have a T.V. in the home.

Two months down the road mama went out of town and we were at my Aunt Shirley's house. Aunt Shirley and my Mother were sisters. We stayed there for a few days. When we got home we found out that someone had broken into our house and stole our only television. We were so disappointed to hear that. They turned the house into a mess. When mama got home she went to call the police. I thought that the police would find our television, and the people who did this, but they didn't.

I often remember mama being sad, and sorrowful. Still telling us that she loved us but she wanted to go home. I didn't understand what she was saying, because she was already at home. (John 14:2.) I wished that daddy would come and live with us so mama wouldn't be so sad and alone all the time. Mama would drink vodka and tell us stories of how she grew up on a chicken farm while living with her aunt Mandy. After living with her mama and her eight siblings, she would long for all of them. Bay-Bay would seem to understand her sadness more than Doris or I could. There was a special bond between mama and Bay-Bay. That was a bond that I couldn't understand at all, until I became an adult.

WHAT HAD ALIENATED US FROM DADDY?

Sometimes daddy would come into town from New York, with a lot of dresses and clothes. Well wouldn't you know it, mama gave some to the girls next door. Every time Daddy came into town, he would go into the bathroom and ask mama for the bottle of alcohol. Later he would seem to be so sleepy, yes sleepy to the point that he couldn't stay awake. It was as if he never got enough rest. Mama would never let us go to New York to visit him. She said that it would be dangerous for us to go to New York. She didn't want daddy's friends to know how his daughters looked. Well we didn't quite understand what mama meant by this. We just trusted her words.

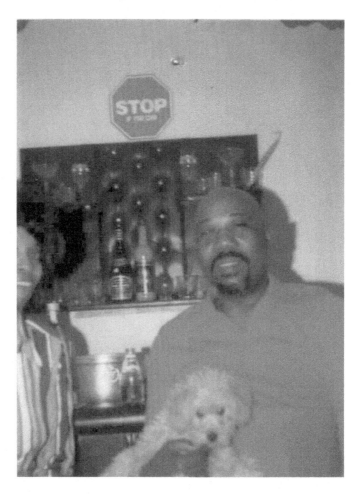

Seeing daddy when I was young made my little heart beat with excitement. Daddy would do magic tricks, and all of the neighbors' kids would gather around him. Being in my daddy's presence would make me shy and nervous. Daddy would show us different versions of these tricks. He looked like me too, even though he was a darker version of me and my sisters. I just thought it was strange that we all including daddy looked so much alike. We didn't know our grandmother on my daddy's side of the family. We didn't know his brothers and sisters either. Daddy would always say that his family was in South Hill. I use to think that it was somewhere out of town or a long ways away. I found out later that South Hill was fifteen minutes away in the city of Chesapeake. Not too far from us at all.

I do remember his aunt, who we called Aunt Nadia. Daddy would take us over to see her when he came into town. I loved Aunt Nadia and she loved us three girls also. She always had open arms for us girls, as well as Bow, who was mentally disabled and in a wheel chair. Aunt Nadia took good care of him as well. She was the only member of daddy's family that we have ever met. We found out later on in life that his mother, sister and brothers were living.

MY FIRST EXPERIENCE WITH DEMONIC FORCES

It was in the year of 1967. I was ten years old, and can recall having what I thought were bad dreams, but they were somewhat different than dreams. It was as if I was awake but I couldn't talk. The atmosphere in the house was illuminated with this fearful and cold chilling presence. I could feel the devil coming into the room, and sitting on the edge of the bed. I could really feel the bed go down as if some one was sitting on it.

I was then tormented with the feeling and experience of something <u>piercing in my stomach</u>. This was so painful. This thing that I couldn't describe would get on top of me and put so much pressure on me that I couldn't breathe. I would try to cry out for help" but I couldn't make a sound. After it was over I was in tears, and very weak. I remember telling my mama about the bad dreams, or episodes. Whatever they were, I was trying to explain to her what had happened, because this was not the first time that this had happened. I needed my mama to help me. I then realized that my sisters had also experience similar episodes as well. **The thief cometh not, but to steal, and to kill, and to destroy: I am come that they might have life, and that they might have it more abundantly. (John 10:10)**

My first experience with the word of God

Mama seemed to always have the answer to all of life's problems. She humbly told us to say The Blood of Jesus. **And they overcame him by the blood of the Lamb, and by the words of their testimony. (Rev. 12:11)** As these episodes would start to begin, (if we couldn't speak at all), to utter The Blood of Jesus in our mind. I couldn't believe it, but it worked. As I was being tormented by this evil force, once again, whether I was asleep or not, I don't know. But I remembered mama telling me to say the blood of Jesus, and I did. I must admit even as a child I was amazed at the results, because the devil left me alone. This was also in the year of 1967.

Mama used to send us to church with our older cousin Louise. We use to walk to Berkley to a near by Church. I didn't understand what the pastor was saying but I use to love being in that atmosphere. I didn't know why the people were crying, and some of them were making strange noises. I often wondered if they were hurting and needed a doctor. My sisters and I would go to church at other times without my cousin Louise. We would buy candy with the money mama told us to put in church. We knew this was wrong but this was our secret.

Mama would send us to vacation bible school as well. **Suffer the little children, and forbid them not, to come unto me; for of such is the kingdom of heaven. (Matthew 19:14)** I can still remember the smell of the church. We had Kool-Aid and vanilla wafer cookies as snacks. I enjoyed the bible stories. I knew that children were very important to God, and that God loved children very much. We sang songs like Jesus loves me yes I know because the bible told me so. We also sung other songs, but that was my favorite song as a child. **For God so loved the world, that he gave his only begotten son, that whosoever believeth in him should not perish, but have everlasting life. (John 3:16)**

I can remember mama reading her Bible sometimes. It was a white Bible. I remember one day opening her Bible and trying to read it, and boy was I confused. The words just didn't make sense to me. Neither did the preacher make any sense to me when I would go to church, for that matter.

But I loved vacation bible school, and sometimes when we got to church early enough, we would participate in Sunday school. I liked that because I understood that a little better than church.

Well it was time for baptism at the church. Grown ups as well as children were going to be baptized. I knew from what I seemed to understand at the church that if I got baptized, then I would get to know God better. I really wanted to know God better.

I also wanted to know Jesus and understand why the people in church would make those noises and cry. Also why did it seem like the preacher was yelling and seeming to be angry sometimes. I thought if I got baptized God would help me to understand these things. Nor did I understand why Mama was so sad so often. Even though I didn't understand these things I still wanted to know about this God. I did know that I felt good when I went to church, and I understood that God loved children so much that He sent His only son to pay for our wrong doings. I knew that God was real when mama told me to plead the blood of Jesus, and the devil left me alone that night. (1 Corinthians 13:11) **When I was a child, I spoke as a child; I understood as a child, I thought as a child . . . (1 Corinthians 13:11)**

So I told mama that I wanted so much to be baptized. She was so glad about it, so she asked Doris and Shirley if they wanted to be baptized as well and they said not yet. Anyway momma dressed me in all white on that night. I can remember my white ruffle socks, this long white robe and this white clean rag tied on my head. I felt like God's little princess. Me, mama, Doris and Shirley went on our way to church. Mama was so proud, and Doris and Shirley were looking at me like I was crazy to be willing to go under all that water,

I remember being in line, waiting to be baptized, and the smell of the water. It smelled so clean, and so different from other water. Well it was my turn now, and the pastor held my hand as I began to step down on the steps. I continued to take steps down in the water. As the water got deeper and deeper it started to feel warm. I can remember putting my trust in God, and the pastor, for not letting me drown. The pastor held me firmly and told me to hold my breath after he finished praying on the count of three. I can recall being submerged under the water. It was so warm but I couldn't hear. This underwater thing was a little scary, but I trusted God even more, because he didn't let me drown.

For some reason when I came out of the water I felt that it was all worth it, and that I was never to forget that night. Doris, Bay-Bay and Momma were so proud of me, but this still didn't make my sisters want to go into that water. At home this was the talk of the week.

Yet mama would continue to drink, as life would seem to be hard for her. While in her endeavor to find God through his word, there was no NIV version of the Bible scriptures at that time. Her getting understanding without any cross references to the scriptures wasn't much help in her quest as she sought to find healing and deliverance for her sadness. Mama continued to believe in God, and to go to Saint Thomas church. She also visited other churches with her sisters. She knew that by her keeping her faith in Jesus Christ that somehow she would eventually be alright.

Signs of Depression in prior family members

I can recall on some Sundays we would get ourselves dressed up and go over to Uncle Eddie B's house. He was always in the bed. I can't recall seeing him out of the bed or ever dressed in clothes. Uncle Eddie B always seemed to have low energy. My aunt Shirley said that he use to be employed at a local shipyard. I do recall Uncle Eddie B giving us girls and his other nieces a cookout in the back yard. His wife Aunt Hattie would host the cook out while Uncle Eddie B would still be in the bed. Yet I still loved uncle Eddie B who was my big momma's brother.

I use to love sleeping with big mama. We would get on our knees to say our goodnight prayers, and she would pray for all of her children. She would also pray for protection from the evil one as well. But most of all she would call God all these great names and tell Him how much she loved him. Then we would get into bed. There was a thick string which was tied to the light switch in the ceiling which also extended and tied to her bed post. She would pull the string, once we were in bed to cut off the light. I could smell the freshness of her bed pillowcases and linens.

I was later reminded by Shirley (Bay-Bay) of the time when we went over to big mama's house; as young children, she would not open the door to let us in. We looked through the window and saw her getting a drink from a small cabinet. We continued to knock on the door, but she wouldn't acknowledge that we were there. It was then, that we walked and told Uncle Eddie, Mama and other family members. No one had a telephone in their home at that time. We told them that big momma was acting strange. When they finally got her to open the door, she said that she felt so sad and sorrowful. She said that she loved us, but she did not want to see or talk to any one. After all big mama worked very hard to support her nine children; she didn't even make three dollars in a week. I choose to clearly remember my big mama as the awesome praying woman that she was.

Pain and hard times in the lineage

Big Mama's first husband Joseph Atkins didn't make enough revenue to totally support the family. Neither was he a family man toward the union he had with big mama and their children. He wouldn't give them anything to eat. He would sit and eat his dinner right in front of them. They had to wait until big mama got home from work to fix dinner for them. After walking home from the cold weather in the winter season herself she would have to put coal in the stove for warmth because my grandfather wouldn't even do that. Neither would he let the children who were of age put coal in the stove to keep warm, whether he was at home or not.

And most of the time he was not at home. My grandfather had another family and other siblings living not too far from my grandmother. My mama and her siblings didn't find out about this other family until they were all grown up. And my big mama wouldn't let them say one negative word against their daddy as they were growing up.

Mama and her siblings had to keep on their coats most of the time in the winter seasons until big mama came home from work to heat the house. My mama and her sisters had to make their skirts out of potato sack bags; she said that the bags came in pretty colors.

They would wash the skirts and starch them to wear to school. Aunt Shirley, my mama sister, who Bay-Bay was named after, would go under the neighbor's house and take a brick to crack walnuts to eat because she was so hungry. They each had to wait their turn to receive a new pair of shoes each month. Joseph Atkins would beat them for any possible reason he could find. He would also beat his only son who was named after him. My mama's only brother, they called him (brother.) We called him Uncle Joe. My mama and her siblings were so afraid of their dad.

If I knew before hand, what I know now about my grandfather, I wouldn't allow another newborn male in my lineage to carry his last name. I believe that your name should carry weight and it should speak for your character. **A good name is rather to be chosen than great riches, and loving favor rather than silver and gold. (Proverbs 22:1).**

During the month of August, we would always celebrate big mama's birthday. It would be a joyous family reunion with all the aunts, uncle and cousins. We had so much food and fun. Everyone was alive and full of life except for Joseph Atkins, my big mama's first husband, who passed away before I was born. These memories of sharing big mama's birthday and all of our family reunions shall continue to be in my memories forever.

GROWING PAINS

———————•◦❊◦•———————

Later on we relocated to Diggs Park, project housing for people with fixed income. I really liked living there because no-one else broke into our house ever again. This project housing had swing sets right in the back yard. Wow we had swings; we never had swings before.

It was during this time of my life that I heard someone calling me. I thought it was mama calling me from the next room over. I answered her but she said "I didn't call you." So I laid down again, a few minutes later someone called me again. I answered. This time mama was not in the next room. This was weird or should I say scary because I know what I heard. Someone was calling me by my name and yet no one was there. Mama said to me the next time this happens, to respond by saying "yes Lord here I am." (1st Samuel 3:4-8) I didn't find out until later in my adult life through the scriptures and prophecy, that there was indeed a calling on my life from God. (Jeremiah 1:5)

As teenage girls the three of us grew even closer, and mama was still over protective of us. Mama never stopped talking to us concerning school, boys, babies, drugs, and life altogether. We couldn't go to any of the parties until we were seventeen years of age. But around the age of fifteen and sixteen we were trying new things that mama would not approve of like cigarettes, pot, and sometimes liquor. We only tried these things when we knew that mama was asleep. Bay-Bay only tried pot once. It didn't agree with her at all. Yet Doris and I smoked until our adulthood. We didn't know that one day the three of us would have a relationship with Jehovah God through Jesus Christ.

I WASN'T PREPARED FOR THIS STORM

———————————•❖•———————————

Mama continued to be sad at times, but still showing much much love for the grandchildren. They were her heart. I can remember her putting her hands on my stomach, some seven years later, telling me that I was pregnant again. I was twenty seven years old at the time. I didn't know; but she knew. And a few months later Mama passed away, after being accidentally dropped down a few steps by her boyfriend as he was trying to put her to bed. He loved her dearly; however, sometimes he had too much to drink as well. I wasn't home at the time, because I had moved out. I was living in the Lakeland area of Norfolk, with my oldest daughter and her father. I wish I had not moved out. Deep down I felt that I should have continued to live at home with mama, knowing that she did drink often. But I was ok with the fact that her boyfriend would take care of her when he didn't have too much to drink. The oldest grandchild was seven years old when mama passed away. We were all so devastated. Oh so much pain. I never thought this kind of pain exist in life. I thought that I was in a bad dream and looking for someone to wake me up, but no one did. We were three young women trying to raise our own children, needing so much direction.

Shirley (Bay-Bay) was so devastated she could not keep her job at Leigh hospital. during this time, Doris and I had no interest in finishing high school. I was so angry with God. I dropped out of high school three times before completing the general course to get my high school diploma. It took me three extra years later to receive the diploma I still give God praise for it today.

I thought the answer to my financial problems was to keep a job, not realizing that I needed more than a job to take care of my little girls. I needed some more schooling. I needed a degree. I also needed my mama, it was to the point that I wanted to die than live without her. I couldn't believe that God would take someone so dear to me. How could God love me? I believe that I hurt for every person in the world, who would ever lose his or her mother.

When my mama passed, I was seven months pregnant with my second child. I had just moved out of my mama's house less than a year ago. I was so angry at God. I was angry at myself for leaving home. But I never thought that she would have an accident down the stairs. I was so sorrowful; I did not think that I would make it at all in life. When I went to the hospital to give birth to my youngest daughter, by

C-section, I remember waking up and talking to God. I asked Him the very question. How could you allow me to hurt like this by taking my mother from me?

He answered me so plainly in my spirit. He said I am God, I give life and I take life, (Job 1:21) and that all of our lives on earth was in His timing, (Ecclesiastes 3:2.) Shortly afterwards the nurse came in to bring me the baby, and laid it down beside me. As this was happening, my children's father walked in the door. Both of us marveled, because it was like my mother being reborn. But this time through my womb, for the baby was the splitting image of my mother.

I never saw that kind of fear come on the kid's dad that way before. I never knew that a child could look so much like the grandmother. My sisters Doris, Shirley, and a host of other guests came to visit the new baby and me. My best friend Rosa; who was babysitting my oldest daughter came by to see the new baby girl. Kentarsha was so proud of her new sister. Of course we named the baby Kenita Deloris Atkins. Deloris is my mom's middle name and my first name. My twin sister Doris was happy about that name, because her oldest son name was Kentorah. Wow what a lot of K's. Therefore after all the guests were gone home, the room was very quiet and the Lord spoke to me again. This time it was clearer in my spirit, letting me know that we are all his creation. Even though we belong to each other, we ultimately belong to Him. **"Behold all souls are mine; (says the Lord) as the soul of the father, so also the soul of the son is mine" (Ezekiel 18:4)** This was letting me know that my mother was not just living through my baby, that she was also living through me as well, (genetic). I didn't understand fully what He meant till later on in life. For the first time since my mothers passing I felt a sense of peace within, knowing that my mother was finally at peace. I knew that God was even more real than I ever knew before, because God gives you a sense of peace within. God gives you a sense of peace and reality that you know that you know without a doubt.

Even as my youngest daughter began to grow up, she still looked and acted so much like my mother. She listened to music my mama listened to. She even dances like my mother used to dance. I see so much of my mama in Kenita. Kentarsha loved her new baby sister so much, and the girls continued to grow in the same love that mama taught us to grow in. I was living in Lakeland apartments in Norfolk at this time, I was still grieving over mama in the seventh year of her passing, but I knew that God was still in control and healing my broken heart as I increased in more of His word.

ABOUT HER FATHER'S BUSINESS

I remember a young lady by the name of Evelyn. She was only about two years older than I was. She had pecan brown skin and was a beautiful young lady. I never knew her last name, but she always wore white. Yes everything she wore was white, even her shoes. She would always ask me to go to church with her, or she would minister to me concerning the gospel of Jesus Christ. It was ok to hear what she had to say but I rejected the offer of going to church with her often. I had no interest in church, yet it was her persistence in her endeavor to reach me, that would get me to the point of running the opposite way when I saw her. One day I saw her coming in my direction, as she was walking down the street, so I hid behind a tree. I remember saying that I can't keep running from her, this has to stop. Even though she wouldn't give up asking me to go to church, I came from behind the tree. She saw me, and as she walked closer to me, she asked the ultimate question after speaking to me. She asked," when are you going to church with me?" This time I said yes. I could tell she was surprise to hear me answer yes. I knew that this was my only way out of having not to run and hide from her anymore, for she was indeed about her Father's business. She was an angel sent from heaven. (Acts 10:3)

THE INTRODUCTION OF GOD'S SOVEREIGN POWER

So I did go to church with her, it was on a Wednesday night. My youngest daughter was four months old and Kentarsha, my oldest was seven years old. I was twenty-eight years old. There was another lady in the car with us, and she also had her young baby with her as well. We went to church that evening and the service was nice. The pastor called an altar call, and the young lady that was with us went to the altar. This was after the service, and she was the last one the preacher had prayed for. I was watching her baby and my own. There was a moment, as I looked at the altar, that the preacher laid his hand on her, and she fell to the floor. She experienced no pain as she ended up on her back. As he continued to pray for her, her body began to lift up off of the floor. I could see the space that separated her body from the floor. As I continued to gaze at this supernatural event, (Acts 1:9.) I remember hearing a voice say to me, "don't ever forget this." And I never forgot what I saw, and what I heard that night.

I marveled in my thoughts concerning this episode, yet it was two months down the road and a friend of mine ask me to go to a party with him. I didn't feel like going but I went anyway. When we entered the house which was in the Park place section of Norfolk, I realized that these people were from a different breed of people that I would normally party with. Because they were a bit on the wild side, I didn't have a chance to even sit down. Then I heard the voice of the lady who went to church with us two months ago. She was in the kitchen, trying to tell the people about her experience at church, and how the Spirit of God lifted her up off of the altar as she experienced the presence of God.

I recall the people saying to her, you are a D . . . lie, and you have had too much to drink. At that time my friend escorted me into the kitchen where they were. She saw me and said with the loud voice, "Oh my God she was there, she was there, she was there, tell them that I am not lying and this did happen." Everyone in the house got quiet and I could only tell the truth, which is what she was telling them anyway. They just didn't believe her because she had been drinking. But after I gave witness to what she was trying to explain, I could see the expressions on their faces, which gave them something to really think about.

I told my friend that I was ready to leave. I never even sat down or had a drink myself. I never saw the young lady or my friend to this day. I know now that I was to witness and to bear witness to God's sovereign power.

FACING SOME HARD CHALLENGES IN LIFE

Well a few years down the road, I faced some challenges in life in being a single mom. I went through more storms than sunshine in the relationship with my kids' father, as well. The fact remain that I alone had to ultimately care for my two girls. I sometimes felt afraid, because I knew that if I didn't make it happen it wouldn't happen. I had to deal with household bills, food, car maintenance, doctors' appointments, the girl's behavior and grades in school. As growing youth, I had to understand their personal problems that occur in their lives. I had to give them guidance in these areas while giving and showing them much love as I tried to set good examples for them to follow, yet sometimes the examples I set was not so positive during those times.

I could no longer keep up the overhead of my apartment alone, so I lived with my youngest sister Shirley for a couple of years. I landed a job at a nearby shipyard; I had to put a plan in motion. I needed to start back over, after losing my apartments for the second time, and get my own place. After the final break up with the kids' father, Shirley did everything to help me to do just that. She had two children herself, Romono and Jon' shay. She bunked her son and daughter in one bedroom, and gave me and my girls the other bedroom. I will always be so grateful to her for that. Her children never complained, and the kids got along as well as we could expect. Of course they fought each other sometimes, but we saw that the love was still there. After all they didn't fight as much as we did as children.

Is there a connection with this sad feeling and my daddy?

———— ◈ ————

But wouldn't you know it. I brought a car after walking and catching a ride to and from work, and now it was time to save some money for my apartment again. I managed to do that too, while even in the midst of partying, gambling, and getting high. I was able to save up some money, and shortly I got my apartment on Chesapeake Boulevard in Norfolk. I was still partying, dating, and getting high. I always felt sad because of wanting my daddy's affection and attention. There was a void missing inside of me. Still remembering when I was a little girl wearing training panties, it was then when my daddy held me in the mirror with him and told me that I was his little girl. Showing me how much I looked like him and how much he loved me, it was then I felt so protected in his arms. A certain bond took place in a split second. I really felt connected and I loved my daddy in a special way. I loved my dad and my mother. I knew that my mother loved me so much, and that she would never ever leave me. But I felt the need to be apart of daddy's life and daddy being apart of my life.

As time went on I saw less and less of him. I was hurt because daddy was never there. His not being there left me with the feeling of rejection that would result in a broken heart. I didn't know how to deal with this kind of pain. When I was a young girl, I would cry sometimes when I was alone, as a child, a young teen, and later as an adult.

I didn't want to share this with Shirley and Doris because I didn't want them to think I was strange or something. I was crying and feeling sad over something that I never had anyway. I wanted to feel loved by my daddy.

ALL GROWN UP AND STILL CRYING FOR MY DADDY?

———•◈•———

I still felt incomplete without my daddy being a part of my life. I couldn't believe it. After all mama had done for me and being there for me, I was still crying and hurt because daddy wasn't there. I often prayed that I would have a relationship with my daddy and that one day we would go to church together and worship God together.

Somehow I felt that if only that could happen, than that would make up for all the hurt and pain that I had encountered over the years. But I continued to cry for my daddy's love, and the relationship that a daughter should have with her dad. I continued to date older men in my young adult life, hoping that the relationship would be just more than a fly by night situation. But it was just that, meaningless. I guess I was trying to fill this void that was missing within me.

I MET A WONDERFUL MAN

——•⊛•——

I met a few men at the shipyard, as well as my best friend who told me about the job at the shipyard.

While working at the shipyard I met another man. There was something different about this one. He was so kind to me and my girls. I felt so safe with him. I knew that I could trust him around my girls. This was a mother's intuition, and wisdom. He made sure that I and my girls were never in need of anything. He was so helpful and caring toward us, even though I didn't see him that much. Now and then I would go out with him. He was surely a gentleman. He opened the car door and all other doors for me. He treated me so special and showed so much concern about my children's welfare. I began to see how wonderful he really was. Yet he was in no way perfect.

I was still tired of the party life, and because I didn't know anything else to do to have fun, I suggested that he and I go to some clubs. To celebrate Halloween night we would dress up and go to the parties. I was still sad a lot and feeling low on energy.

Our relationship was off and on at times because of the indecisiveness on both of our part. There were break-ups, in between the relationship. Who wanted to get serious anyway? I just had no more energy to date or to party. I just went to work and raised my two girls.

WHAT IS THIS AWFUL SAD FEELING?

———•❀•———

I remember getting off to work one day, and I stopped pass my Aunt Shirley's house. I recall opening up to her about these feelings, because at this point I needed some wisdom or light on this subject matter. I felt so tired and sad most of the time. I had no interest in things. As I was explaining myself to her, and observing her response to me, I then realized that she had no clue of what I was trying to convey to her. I found out later that this was depression that I was experiencing. I later discovered that neither she nor my late mother or their other siblings knew a thing about depression, yet they had experienced the same feelings.

As time went on, I began to go to New Hope Church in Norfolk. I felt led to take my girls with me and on a couple of occasions my friend Harvey. Harvey and I met at the shipyard.

As time went on and these bad feelings had gone, I begin to party again, date again and get high. But through all of this I never stopped going to church because it made me feel better. Even when I didn't get a full revelation of what the pastor was saying, I just went because I knew that it made me feel better. This is how I knew that God was real. I didn't know there could be more to God than just going to church, and feeling good afterward.

I MARRIED THIS WONDERFUL MAN

As time went on I continued seeing the nice gentleman, Harvey T. Allen Jr. more often than I would see any other man. I guess it was because he treated my girls as if they were his own. He even introduced me and my kids to his mother and his kids. And wouldn't you know it; his girls' names are Karen and Karnita. And my girls' names are Kentarsha and Kenita. OK here we go with the K's again. He also has a son whose name is Harvey. Later I would meet his other daughter Sonya.

This time we dated and things got serious. I felt that he was going to ask me to marry him. After dating on and off for two years, wouldn't you know it, he got on his knees and asked me to marry him. Oh my God I was so excited; I never had a proposal before. Nor have I ever been engaged before. Harvey and I began to fall in love, even though I felt that we were not compatible. But somehow, in this case, opposites did attract. And more so, we were good for each other and with each other.

We got married on March 30, 1992. My cousin Bubba gave me away to the groom at my wedding. A small wedding with only immediate family and the pastor of New Hope COGIC church who officiated the ceremony. I thought that if I got married in a church that God would always be the head of my marriage, because this choice to get married would be a serious change in me and my girls' lives. I was still sad because daddy couldn't find the time to give me away nor was he even at the wedding. There would be times while in the bed with my husband, after he was asleep, I would turn my back to him and silently cry for my daddy. This went on for years.

THE DEVASTATING PASSING OF
MY DEAR FRIEND

Harvey and I both worked at the local shipyard. Some five years after our marriage, my best friend, who told me about the hiring at the shipyard, had gotten killed a few months after I was married. She was killed by her ex-boyfriend. I was devastated, and tormented by her sudden death. When I thought that I had already experienced the abundance of pain when I suddenly lost my mama, this was just too much to bear. While trying to be strong for her children and family, I realized that her sudden death was too much for me to handle, as well as the details of what really happened that night. I wasn't there at the birthday party that night because I was a new wife and I was trying to stay home with my new husband and my daughters, for a change. It was my way of helping this new change in my life. I wish I was there at the party. Maybe things would have been different, or maybe I could have somehow saved her life. Of all times I wasn't there. I wasn't there for her. Now I still keep in touch with her kids as well as her mother and father as much as I can. The Lord is still healing, because there was a time that I couldn't talk about this at all.

What a scandal

⋯⊛⋯

I took a leave of absence from the shipyard to have some eye surgery. This way I could stay home for a while. After losing my best friend of seventeen years. I needed the rest.

Shortly after that I went back to work. I wasn't back for long before there was another incident. This time with one of my managers. I reported my issues to the personnel department, only to find out that it made matters worse. What a scandal, what a mess. It was all over the shipyard. I just wanted him to stop mistreating me and putting me on the night shift whenever he got ready. Maybe I should have handled this another way or could I have been sending the wrong signals? I was still longing for my daddy, and wanting a father's love; I was still grieving over the lost of my best friend of seventeen years, and longing for my mother. I was still this sad person on the inside.

Also there were some problems arriving in my marriage at this time. Where was my mind? As people began to talk about my scandal and gossip about it, life began to be too much for me to handle at the time. I couldn't even drive my car because of my lack of concentration. I would be driving down the street to point A and find myself at point B, or even sometimes arriving at Point C. I couldn't even concentrate on the street signs or lights. My twin sister, Doris would drive me around to do my chores while my husband was at work, so he wouldn't have to do it when he got off from work. I was on short term released from work at the shipyard by my doctor.

Yet even to this day, I never forgot to thank God for the soundness of mind. However I didn't stay at the shipyard, I left shortly afterward in 1996, after being diagnose with post traumatic stress disorder, and I was told that I would always have this condition. That's what man say.

WOMEN SHOE STORE, BEING A BLESSING

•◦❀◦•

I then went into the shoe business with my oldest daughter, Kentarsha. She was always a business lady, and the Lord had blessed this business for seven years. She always had a dream of opening a woman's shoe store. By the fifth year of the shoe business, we were located at Providence Rd. in the Chesapeake area of Virginia right beside the big Farm Fresh grocery store. I enjoyed ministering to the women, giving them literature, and often praying with them in the back room. Sometimes someone would come in the store to give me a word from the Lord and pray for me as well. We also had a shoe store on Campostella road, where the old giant open-air grocery store was located. The lines were wrapped around the inside of the store; these women loved shoes. The Lord had given me a vision to bring mothers and daughters together by incorporating Ma-Ma Tar boo's Shoes, where the heels were lower, and the styles were a little conservative than the younger women shoes. Truly our shoes brought mothers and daughter together in a closer bond and they shopped together in Tar boo's Diva Spot, Shoe Store. It was during this time that the Lord blessed me with his promise of a Rav4 Sports utility van. He promised this to me years ago. Therefore I dedicated the vehicle back to the Lord with promises that I would use it for his glory and his glory alone. I got special plates that read GDS SUV.

By the time of my seventh year of marriage, I continued to thirst and hunger for the word of God even more. I knew that the only way that I could deal with the ups and downs, and the trials of life, was to keep this relationship with God. It made me feel so much better. Often times I was awakened by the Lord all times of the morning. As He ministered to me, I would spend time with the Lord at his request, or my longing for it.

My relationship with God seemed confusing to close friends and family, because I couldn't stay stable in this relationship with God. I didn't know how to be delivered from the things that I was doing in the world. My family and friends would say from time to time, "there she goes, she is saved again." I would try to stay away from my own sin nature, as being obedient to God, but I never had the power to do so.

I can remember going to some home bible studies at Deaconess Jones house, and watching God in other people. Seeing the fruit of their spirit, and seeing something so different about them, I knew that I was craving a cigarette the minute the bible studies were over, and as far as I knew there was no glow in me. I wondered if something this wonderful could ever happen to me like I saw happen in others.

But I wanted so much to be washed and cleaned spiritually, and to have that glow the way they did. I wanted God to use me for His glory. Any way He wanted to do it was alright with me, I knew that there had to be more to life than this.

THE EVENING OF DELIVERANCE AND TRIUMPHANT

I can remember one night talking to one of the saints of God on the phone. Knowing that she was an ex drug dealer, and a former childhood best friend, she is saved, sanctified and filled with the Holy Ghost. She is also a first lady who married her first love. We both dated our kids' father at the age 17 years old.

And now she has the evidence of speaking in other tongues and ministering to me with this awesome anointing. After I finished talking with her, I said that I was going to be all that God had pre ordained me to be as well. Therefore I immediately got down on my knees, admitting to God that I know with every fiber of my being that He was the ultimate High God, Jehovah God. And that I know like I know my name, that He put the sun, moon, and stars in the sky. And that no man has done these things. I know that He was able to deliver me from my sinful nature, which hindered me from being a faithful witness to someone else for His glory. I was not going to get up off of my knees until he delivered me, because I had the faith to know that He would and could do just that (Hebrews 4:16).

I told God that this was just a small thing for him to do. He had already created the universe. I cried out to God from the depth of my heart for this change. Wouldn't you believe it? He gave me a check in my spirit. Something awesome happened to me while on my knees that I still can't quite convey to you in words. But I pulled myself up on the couch, and then angels began to fill the room. I just know that they were angels. It was a joyous time; a time of celebration. It was a real party. But this party was different, and special. There was music in my heart as the atmosphere was somehow illuminated with the presence of the Lord. For the host of this party was the Lord of Lords and the King of Kings. He was the honored guest; He really came to the party. He and His angels, and they ministered to me as I lifted my hands and worshiped Him. I was overwhelmed by being in His presence (Luke 15:10) (Luke 15:7).

It was so wonderful! And I did get high. But this time the high was a spiritual high. A high that was better than any high that I ever had. This felt better than any substance or intimacy that I had ever experienced in my life. It lasted for a whole week. I knew then that I was no longer going to give my money to the drug dealer or the cigarette company. I used to love to smoke and smoke, and smoke, until it was coming out of the pores of my skin. I could smell it even though I hadn't smoked that particular day. I knew that if I continued to pray and study God's word then I could always have this intimacy with the Lord. That was far greater than my experience with any human being. And knowing this, I know that I will please him in every way, bearing fruit in every good work. (Colossians 2:9).

TEMPTATION AFTER TRUE SALVATION

---·•◉•·---

A few hours later, the cravings for the cigarettes came back, this time stronger that ever. I was moved by a power that was not my own. Nor was it the power of God. I went into the kitchen garbage can where I put a pack of cigarettes earlier, knowing that I had poured chicken grease on them earlier. I was tired of smoking after some thirty years. Well I found the cigarette, and I took a napkin to wipe off the chicken grease. I then opened the pack toward the back where the cigarettes had not been touched by the chicken grease. I then was moved to go into the bathroom, because that's where I used to smoke or on the porch when my husband was asleep. Yes through all of this he was still asleep. He didn't hear a thing, so I went into the bathroom and lit the cigarette. I smoked it and smoked it, for it was almost half done. I realized that I never got the nicotine fix that I usually got when I craved cigarettes.

And I heard the Lord speak to me so clear in my right ear. And He said to me in my spirit "you are already delivered." And I heard a chilling voice, so clear say "smoke that cigarette." Oh my God, I thought, this is really happening. I quickly flushed the cigarette in the toilet, went back into my prayer room and got back on my knees. I worshiped God for my deliverance. I guess I was in worship until 2:00am. I was so grateful for what God had done for me. That was the last time I put a cigarette in my mouth. Even though the cravings did come back, and I did go through some withdrawals from this addiction, but God was with me every step of the way. He was ministering to me and teaching me to speak his word to the temptations, and allowing the power of God's word to keep me (Matthew 4:1-11).

A SINCERE ANSWER TO THE CALL

I answered my calling as a minister of the gospel, on September 17, 2002. I attended a church, where the pastor had such an awesome anointing of the revelation of teaching the scriptures. It was there that I got the revelation of who I really was in the Kingdom of God. I was a member in the body of Christ. Jesus has given us power to tread over all the power of the enemy (Luke 10:19).

During this time the Lord would wake me up at unusual times in the morning, and speak to me. He would put things in my spirit, such as M.I.T. with bits and peaces. Until one morning I got the full revelation of this M.I.T, which was being taught at the church by this pastor. He wanted me to attend this class that they offered at church called Ministers in Training.

Well I fainted twice. Yes literally fainted, as God gave revelation to me on this subject. I fainted again the first day entering into this M.I.T. class. The pastor repeated some things that God had already put in my spirit while in my prayer room. I knew that I had this call because of the growing relationship with God, and how he would speak to me.

I was afraid to answer this call, and I really didn't want to do it for being afraid that I would not be able to keep the commitment to the Lord. But I knew that deep inside of me that this is what God wanted me to do. At that time I was afraid not to obey the Lord, and I had to trust him and not lean unto my own understanding, I often wondered to myself how He could find me worthy of this call at all. (Gen. 32:10)

A CALL TO HEALING THROUGH THE WOMEN'S FELLOWSHIP

I continued to cry for my daddy on late nights, even after six years of my marriage. I later joined another Church, where my pastor was one of my childhood friends who played on the asphalt streets with us as kids, in the Campostella section of Norfolk. Oh how God used this man.

This is where I was introduced to the women fellowship ministry. Here is where I found so much healing and deliverance for the hurt and pain that occurred in my early childhood. My mother's drinking and her being sad and lonely all of the time, and the fact that daddy was never there like he should have been. As I listened to other women's testimonies, I begin to be restored, refined, renewed and delivered from the depression as well as the medication that I was told I would be on for the rest of my life. The medication was for the post-traumatic stress disorder. My doctors believed in me as I believed that God had healed me from this mental disorder. (1Peter 2:24)

As I grew in the word of God, and continued to go to these women fellowships, I was able to overcome my depression and the attacks of the enemy, by the blood of the Lamb and the words of my testimony. I began to develop a zeal for the ministry as I experienced the present, and the healing power of God in the midst of each session (Matt. 18:20). Later I became the assistant and then the president of the women's fellowship, and I later began to continue to teach women who were broken and finding it hard for themselves to go on to the next chapter in their lives. Sometimes we can't move on due to past hurt, pain and un forgiveness. Yet I want to obtain the ultimate goal of being that woman by God's grace, that Prude Woman.

MINISTERING REDEMPTION TO MY HURT AND PAIN

L ater on I got in touch with my daddy. After getting my healing and some deliverance in the women's fellowship sessions, I went to see him. It was then that I told him about the benefits of being saved, and neither one of us had to give our money to drug dealers anymore. I told him about the joy of serving God, and how God had taken the taste of drugs and cigarettes out of my spirit. It was this evening that my dad had told me how he was trying to find God, yet he had never committed and received Christ as his Lord and Savior.

He really wanted to do this because he saw the joy that I had, and it had to be more to life than this. Because he himself wanted to be delivered from the drug heroin, which had taken over so much of his life, I asked him if he was ready to do it today. And he said yes. I want Jesus to be Lord and Savior of my life. Therefore I walked him through Salvation by ministering to him (Romans 10:9,) and daddy did receive Christ as the Lord and Savior of his life.

I remember experiencing the joy of the Lord all over him. He appeared to be so vigorous. I was more excited than I was over my first and only bicycle, that Christmas day, with my sisters. I thought I was dreaming, and I never wanted to be awakened from this dream.

The next time that I went to see my daddy, he asked me to forgive him for not being there all of those years. It was as if he knew the hurt that I carried around with me all of those years, I often wondered how he could have known.

I realized that this new relationship with my daddy is what I asked God for. It was really unveiling before my very eyes. Daddy went to church with me on a few occasions, and I would be in amazement as I watched him worship the Lord and then gazing at him as he walked to the altar to give his offering unto the Lord.

Later I would go to his house and read the Bible with him. Wow this is what I remember praying to God some years ago. God has truly answered my prayers. I couldn't believe it. I was so happy and bubbling with excitement, I told my husband that I wanted him to meet my daddy. But the time never presented itself at that time, or anytime for that matter.

A VISIT TO HELL

---•❈•---

What in the world is going on? As time went on I began to see less of daddy. There was a spirit of distance. Something felt so wrong in my spirit. I knew that at that time daddy was still getting high. I remembered Mama said that daddy had gotten injured while fighting in the Korean War in the 1950s. He was still bearing the scars from that war. I felt helpless, as though I was losing a battle. I can remember one Father's Day when Pastor Rouson gave an awesome message. Even though I was sitting in church I could feel my daddy's spirit being tormented. I recall asking my prayer partner, Minister Cherry if she would go to hell with me to pull my daddy out. He needed to be delivered and set free. And she did go with me. As we pulled up into the driveway, we saw drug traffic, and as we prayed and anointed ourselves with olive oil, we began to position ourselves for spiritual warfare.

I recall us going up the steps, because his apartment was on the second floor. There was such a chilling atmosphere. It was different than the drug atmosphere that I had known.

Men were going in, and coming out of his apartment. They were walking in total darkness. We went right in and the house was full of people. Daddy was so high and helpless.

The men wouldn't stop measuring and bagging the drugs even as I was desperately ministering to my daddy one on one. Even though the house was full with drug addicts, I begged daddy to plead the blood of Jesus. I knew there was power in the blood, even if it would not manifest right away. I knew deep in my heart that God could and that He would help my daddy. I had to stay in the spirit with this thing because in the natural it seemed that I was losing this battle.

I prayed as my prayer partner was praying softly in the spirit for me and daddy. He finally told me that he would see me the next day. I realized that he wanted me to leave because he didn't want me to see him that way. He looked so helpless. I did leave, even though I would continue to be prayerful and not lose hope.

But I left this promise to the kingdom of darkness, Satan himself and every demonic force that had been assigned to my daddy's life. The promise was, by my faith in God Almighty, according to Gods immutable word, satan would not have victory in this situation nor will he have my daddy's soul. <u>For this was not over</u>, I declared war unto the kingdom of darkness because God is faithful. He would not allow my daddy to be tempted above that which he was able, without making a way of escape for him through that same temptation. He would save him from hell's bondage the same way that he saved my momma. (1Cor: 10:13). For even in daddy's weakness his faith in God would be counted as his righteousness (Romans 3:25-26) and that God would ultimately heal him from the power of satan and deliver him, (Revelation 21:4). He will allow him to walk in the liberty where Christ has already made him free, when he led captivity captive. (Ephesians 4:7-10)

(John 10:10) Jesus Christ came that we (the believer) might have life and have it more abundantly; therefore we know that in the abundance there is a plenteous and overflow. That overflow of life in Jesus Christ will pass over with our inner man, when our physical body expires here on this side, and our soul passes on into eternity. (John 11:25-26)

SALVATION AT HELL'S DOOR

As we were leaving my daddy's apartment, a man was coming up to my dad's apartment. We met him eye to eye. He looked so tormented. My prayer partner asked him if he wanted to be free. She continued on by telling him about the love of God and that God wanted him to be free from that bondage of drugs and sin. He began to weep; he surrendered his life to Christ. As my prayer partner walked him through salvation, he received Christ on the steps of my daddy's apartment. (Matthew 9:37). He then told us that he was meeting his boss here who was planning to score drugs also. He was so tired of this lifestyle, therefore I prayed for his newfound strength in the Lord. I told him to read the book of John, the last book of the gospels in the Bible, and that the Lord would continue to strengthen him.

He did not go into the house at that point; he had a change of heart. Shortly afterward, his boss did come up to the apartment, and he did go in as we were leaving the stairwell.

I knew by walking this man through salvation, that God was pleased. This was a divine appointment for this man's soul. God would ultimately take care of daddy because the prayers had gone forth to the throne of God and I know that God did hear them (Daniel 10:12). I also knew that when we take care of God's business that God will take care of our business.

DADDY WENT HOME TO BE WITH THE LORD

As time went on I felt in my spirit that daddy was having a hard time. There was never time for us to either go to church together or read the Bible together. There were only memories of those special moments which still seem like a dream to me. But I know that these things did happen. Daddy did give his life to the Lord, he did study and go to church with me, and he did give his offerings unto the Lord. God promises to me came alive.

Less than twelve months later we got a call from his neighbors. They called Shirley (Bay-Bay) and told us that our daddy had been robbed and someone had killed him. Shirley called me and we called Doris. We then went to my daddy's apartment and the neighbors were outside and a detective asked if we were the next of kin. They said that it didn't look like fowl play to them. They told us that daddy had a needle loaded with heron in his hand, preparing to inject it into his arm. But he died before he could do so. They allowed us to go upstairs into his apartment to see him. I couldn't believe that he was gone. I watched him on the floor, and saw some blood by his ear and head. This was all too much for me. I couldn't believe this was happening. We left back out and stood outside. By that time all the spectators had gone and I began to weep. I couldn't hold it in. There was a feeling of this ball inside of my stomach, and it desperately needed to be released. And as I cried out <u>with this final cry</u>, I felt a release of my daddy's spirit. I felt like I had just given birth, I no longer had to carry this. <u>Now</u> I could finally let him go. Daddy died on March 9th 2005, and that was the last time that I have ever cried for my daddy again. After forty-seven years of crying, I don't have to cry or weep any more. I have only tears of joy because of daddy's freedom in Christ. I didn't cry at his home going service either. Later on we got the autopsy report and it stated that daddy died of natural causes. No man took his life. Therefore God did truly make a way of escape for daddy, while using that same temptation. For that dose of heroin never made it inside of his body.

I realized that after all these years, <u>my soul was tied to my daddy's soul</u>, and the tie was released at his departure from this life, Daddy would enter eternity with his high priest and the bishop of his soul. <u>Now</u> not only is daddy free, but I am also free from this soul tie. I know that daddy is healed, delivered and set free. Oh yes, my mama and daddy shall indeed live forever in that great mansion (John 14:2). Now I am free to go forth with God's commissions and assignments for my life, knowing that I shall one day have a room in that mansion as well.

Meltdown of major depression

This was a time of winding down for my daughter and my shoe store. I worked as the general manager for six years. I had been working with and for my oldest daughter Kentarsha. This was her dream since high school to have a ladies shoe store. The store was named Tar boo's, which was her nick name when she was a little girl. My best friend who suddenly passed away while we were both employed at the shipyard gave her this nick name at a very young age. The business was doing really well for six years. We met so many women and they loved us as much as they loved the shoes. We even took pictures of them trying on and buying shoes. We would put the pictures around the counter where they could see themselves. We made them feel as special as they were.

We even did some television commercials for the shoe store; we put my first granddaughter Amore in some of the commercials when she was about five months old. We were selling baby girl shoes at that time as well.

I would find myself praying and ministering to most women as the Lord would lead them into the store. Some of them thought that they were coming to buy shoes. Then they would open themselves up to me in conversation as though they had always known me.

A few of them gave their lives to the Lord, right in the back room of the store, where we kept our refrigerator and back stock. I would even make flyers of encouraging words to put on the counter for the women. Sometimes they would just peep their head in and ask, what do you have for me today? Because each week they knew there was a fresh word from the Lord. What a beautiful time of bonding together for women and young girls, mothers and daughters. We were also making money.

Then there came a season of quietness. Not just in the store but in my spirit as well. I began to feel stressed and distance from the Lord. I had a feeling of being oppressed. I felt like I had awaken one day, and the whole world was on top of me.

I was trying to look at my children, husband, health, and bills to find a reason why I would feel this way. My new doctor ran any and every test on me because I was a new patient. One of the test was called a cat scan. I knew they saw something when the nurse had this funny look on her face when she came in with the pictures of all of my inside organs.

Later the doctor told me that I had a spot on my liver, (**the same place that I was pierced in the stomach, as a child by demonic forces**). It would take me two weeks to get further test done, and two weeks to get the results. I would need to make an appointment with him a week after I took the final test. That would finalize this spot on my liver; it took me one month and one week to get the final test results. This was the longest month in my life. I had to war like never before. Some days I was just too tired to war in the spirit. I could only speak a word to the situation. I had to also speak to the spirit of fear (Ps.23: 4). The devil spoke all kinds of negativity to my mind, as the spirit of fear would grip me to my wits end. But God was faithful, for He was indeed with me every step of the way. He allowed my ministering angels to minister peace to me (Hebrews 1:14) through the word of God.

Will someone come and pray for me? That's what I was thinking each time I went to church. I finally told my Pastor, and she said that she was going to speak with me concerning my continence. She said that the Lord had already told her to pray with and for me. This woman of God looked me in the eyes and asked me to look her in the eyes. What beautiful, brown anointed eyes. And when I did as she asked, I saw the peace and the power of God.

My Pastor prayed with authority and with the power that had been given to her by our Lord and Savior, (Luke 10:19). She called out the spirit of fear and replaced it with peace, which is the word of God that Jesus has given every believer. He gives us a peace, which surpasses all understanding. (Ph. 4:7)

This prayer and warfare had totally revived me. I was indeed going to make it. I could endure the longsuffering of waiting for the test results and believing God for life. The Bible tells me to speak life as well as to expect life (Proverb 18:21). Well I went back to the doctor a month and one week later. I wanted to go to the doctor's office alone. No husband, no children and no sisters. I was revived by my pastor's prayers to the point that I was strong enough to bear the answer to the tests. I put my trust in the Lord, as He did go to the doctor with me. Just me and the Lord.

When I got into the doctors office, the doctor had a long list of test results. I didn't know that they did so many tests. The doctor began to read them off in order. I so wished that he would have given me the detrimental news first. I couldn't believe that he was taking his time, and going down this long list, until he got to the spot on the liver. It was then that he said that it was benign. He continued to read down the list of results. When I stopped him and asked him again to be sure that he said benign, clearly meaning no cancer in my body, he said yes. This is benign and there is **No Cancer.**

I don't remember what else he said from that point because I was crying with joy, and giving God glory. The doctor was not emotional at all, nor was he even happy for me. I guess he had to maintain a level of professionalism. I asked him what was the spot on my liver and his response was that it could be a spot of blood. But it was common in most people. I was so relieved and amazed at the favor of God in this physical area of my life. I didn't take it for granted because I knew that some people don't walk out of the doctor's office with a spot on the liver and still have a praise report. I realize that this is the exact spot where I was pierced by the devil as a child, but to God be all the glory.

I later changed doctors, because I wanted and needed a patient doctor relationship with my physician. I felt as though he should have made me feel relaxed by assuring me the good news first. He had to go.

LOSING HER FOCUS

—◦◉◦—

My daughter seemed to be losing focus of the business. This was her dream. I realized that the enemy was coming against her as fear began to creep into the gaps. She would lose her focus on her dream and then direct her focus to other areas in her life that she thought at the time was making her happier. She dreamed of having a ladies shoe store. She also wanted to be that prude woman she so often desired to become.

She would call me throughout the night to pray with her as she began to realize the attack from satan (John 10:10). She now sees satan for what he truly is, and he is a liar and the father of lies.

She began to fall for this younger man. Yes he was literally younger than she was. But that wasn't the problem because she is a grown up after all. But this young man was so handsome, yet he had so many issues. The Lord would use me to minister and pray for him. I had no problem with that, but the problem was that my daughter seemed to be consumed with this young man. She seemed to be so happy with him, even if he couldn't afford to take her out to dinner. He didn't have a career or a job. It was as if the sun rose and set on this young man.

I began to see different spirits operating through him, which was of course, not in agreement with the righteousness of God. In reality it was the opposite. But my daughter seemed to be drawn and controlled by what seemed to be one of the most wonderful relationships she had ever encountered. She realized shortly thereafter that it was a nightmare from hell (he was abusive). But my most desired prayer was that this young man surrendered his life to Christ, and to begin to be transformed by the word of God. Through it all, I could feel his pain and his hurt from his past childhood. I prayed earnestly for my daughter. I warred spiritually on her behalf, because there was indeed a soul tie there that had to be broken.

About six months later the soul tie was broken, and my daughter was delivered from this relationship. She received revelation from the Lord, which she has shared with me. My prayer is that she applies what God has given her so that she may walk in wisdom.

I know that she has given her life to the Lord, but I also pray for transformation in her life through the word of God as well. And it shall come to pass for the both of them in Jesus name.

THE BIRTHING OF HIS AND MY BABY

I recall in prayer and talking with the Lord concerning this relationship with my daughter and the young man. I received this revelation from the Lord; this was not about my daughter, it was about my faith being on trial (1 Peter 1:7). God wanted my faith in the fire. But I didn't know why because God knew that I loved him and would serve him with every fiber of my being. I couldn't believe that God wanted more from me. I thought that this was an attack from the devil. My daughter would have not chosen a man who would treat her unfair or unjust in any way.

But I understood as I communed with the Lord, that God wanted my faith tried in the fire. He wanted to take me to another spiritual level in him, (Rom 1:17) that I may obtain the fullness of the authority and benefits of the Kingdom of God (Matt. 16:19). God was trying to take me somewhere. God was preparing me through my faith for the ministry that he had recently birthed in me, which was the **Keeping Power of the Holy Spirit through the Word of God.** He had given me a **mission** and a **vision** for this ministry. And the **Vision** was to impute sound doctrine into those who find it difficult to walk in the vocation wherein they were called. That they may understand who God is in their lives and who they are in Christ. To put off formality and walk in the Divine power the Lord has already given them; that they might be partakers of Christ Divine nature and having total deliverance in areas that will hinder their spiritual growth. Wow what a vision from on high.

Therefore the **Mission** for this ministry is to administer the immutable word of God through the scriptures, which manifest in the true light of the gospel of Jesus Christ in the hearts of mankind. That they will know the hope of their Holy calling through Christian doctrine, values, and principles, for the purpose of extending holiness through out the world, as it ministers to the temporal as well as the spiritual needs of the individual. It was during this time when God was giving me insight on this matter as well as helping me to get a 501 c3, and to have the ministry incorporated. He showed me a young lady who I only met once at a women's fellowship. I was to give her a call. And I did call her, not knowing how I got her phone number. She didn't remember giving it to me either, but I told her that God had told me to call her. She was to help me with the 501c3 and other paperwork concerning this ministry. She replied and said to me that she knew that this was God and that she would help me. And she did, without charging me one dime. The value of her time and labor for this paperwork cost well over $1500.00. Her name is Minister Lisa

Smith. God sent her all the way from Tennessee to be a wonderful blessing just for me. (Smile).

It was for this cause that my precious faith was being tried, as I have, and will encounter heaviness through manifold temptations while living here on earth (1 Peter 1:6).

A CHANGE IN THE ATMOSPHERE

The women stop coming to buy shoes. It was naturally and spiritually quiet at this time. There was no prayer, which was a good thing because I couldn't pray anyway. They didn't even come for a flyer with an encouraging word because I didn't have that either.

The days began to turn into weeks and the weeks into months. I would do my best to act normal, even though I was feeling far from it. I was so depressed and oppressed, and feeling helpless, that I couldn't pray in the Holy Ghost. Nor could I pray a normal surface prayer, and sometimes I couldn't pray at all. This was unbearable. The lack of energy got to the point that I didn't care if I had on make up or even if my hair was fixed. My husband would ask me sometimes if I felt ok. And my answer to him would sometimes be "not really." But I knew that I couldn't explain to him what was going on, for fear of worrying him. I didn't want him telling me to go back to the doctor and try to get back on the depression medicine. But this feeling was so different and yet so diabolical, for this spirit was soaring with a mission to leave no evidence of life in me.

This experience with depression was somewhat different than the last experience because this one brought on the sense of confusion and fear. I was forced to speak scriptures to address each of these two spirits. Yet there were times when it seemed as if they would never let up, in my soul I felt as if I was waving a white flag of surrender. I was no longer a soldier on the battlefield, yet maybe in the land of shiner somewhere, (Genesis 11:2 & 14:1.) Which is the open bare, low land surrounding Babylon. I felt all alone while lying on my back with no spiritual armor on, as if my co-labors in the army of the Lord did not even know that I was missing in action.

I would continue to go to church to hear the word of God, and watch Christian television programs. By this time the shoe store was taking a deep plunge for the worse.

WHERE DID THE SHOE STORE DREAM GO?

---·•❊•·---

Competition begins to rise from many areas, from the largest to the smallest shoe store. I knew that the season was taking a plunge as we tried desperately to make a come back. Yet, we tried to hold on to the store for dear life, until we both knew that our money was not as long as the major companies.

We did finally receive the truth on this matter. As our competitors would offer real nice shoes for such a lower price, we found it to be an honor that other companies would send their people into our store to check out our styles as well as our prices. What an honor. We must have been doing something right. We later gave all the shoes that we didn't sell to our local church for the children to go back to school.

I was in the process of making the transition from the shoe business, to a secular job. I had no idea that I wouldn't get a job until one year later.

I was working in the church to help feed the unfortunate people in the neighborhoods. The shoe business ended, and we both lost money. For the last six months, there was no money and no shoe store.

I found myself having to do a chapter seven bankruptcy to clear my credit of debt which did not obtain a profit from the shoe store. There was also mismanagement of finances. I had to repent for not being a good steward over my financial affairs, and I asked my daughter to do the same. Both my daughter Kentarsha and I have learned great lessons from these errors.

Our customers had gotten attached to us. We were like one big happy family. There were women of all ages, and nationalities as well. There were also girls in their early teens who were upset that the business had ended.

Uncovering the spirits of Oppression and Depression

As my depression began to increase, it was harder and harder for me to get out of the bed and shower. I did manage to mask my problems for a little while. But this episode was far worst than the other episodes. I didn't really know what to do because I was struggling with the fact of having to go back to the doctor and let them know that the disease was back and worst than before. I had no energy to do anything but mope around the house and talk to God. One day as I was cleaning around the house, I was listening to TBN Ministry. I heard a minister speaking on the subject of wicked forces in the Bible still existing today because satan is still the prince of the air. He was speaking on the name and character of **Nimrod.** As he was speaking on this subject something inside of me began to check, and after the program, within my spirit, I spoke to God. This time I began to receive strength in my sorrowful and weakened spirit. I proceeded to utter the blood of Jesus, as I was also able to utter in tongues and ultimately pray earnestly as minutes went by. And as this was going on, the heaviness that I was feeling began to lift, as if someone had taken the whole world off of me. I felt like I had been taken out of an awful pit, because this spirit was heavy and the depth of it was most defiantly deep.

I did see in the spirit bronze color sand particles, or it could have been crystals deteriorating until it existed no more. I felt restored, revived and strengthened, as I began to praise God like a mad woman. But yet this name **Nimrod** continued to stay on my mind. I asked myself who this Nimrod was. And what was he all about? Well I know that there is a Genesis, or should I say a beginning of everything and everyone.

I began to read Genesis (10:1) and verses where the Bible introduced the generations of the sons of Noah, which were Shem, Ham, and Japheth, and unto them were born <u>sons after</u> <u>the flood</u>, and verses 6-12, tells who their sons were. Verse 6, tells us that the sons of Ham were Cush, and Mizraim, and Phut and Cannan.

Verse 7, says that the sons of Cush were Seba, and Havilah, and Sabath, and Raamah, and Sabtecha, and the sons of Raamah, Sheba, and Dedan.

Verse 8 and 9 gave me this insight of this person **Nimrod,** for Cush begat **Nimrod;** he began to be a mighty one in the earth, for verse 9 indicates that he was a mighty hunter before the Lord, wherefore it is said, even Nimrod the mighty hunter before the Lord.

Now in verse 10, for it reads that the beginning of his kingdom was Babel, and Erech, and Accad, and Calneh, in the land of **Shinar. (Note* in every kingdom there is a ruler which means king).**

Verse 11 says out of that land went forth **Asshur,** and built Nineveh, and the city Rehoboth and Calah, and resin between Nineveh, and Calah; the same is a great city. Asshur was the grandson of **Noah**, the son of **Shem.** Genesis (10:11) says that out of that land went forth **Asshur,** who was the son of Shem operating in the leadership of building **Nineveh**, and the city Rehoboth and Calah. The Assyrian people derived from **Asshur**, who also helped **Nimrod** his cousin, build the tower of Babel in all defiance to **God's laws.** (Babel means confusion) yet Nineveh was the capital of the ancient Assyrian empire.

Colonizing Through Fear = <u>F</u>alse <u>E</u>vidence <u>A</u>ppearing <u>R</u>eal

Note* the two rulers have now colonized their territories in the earth by extending their wicked kingdoms through force <u>or</u> influence by the power of the fallen angels which fell with Satan. And as they transformed each territory, it would manifest their beliefs, culture, nature and evil lifestyle. But Babel was only the beginning of their Kingdoms that their diabolic influence would also try to revolt mankind from the divine laws and authority which they thought would stop the son of God from coming into the world to redeem mankind from the fall which happened in the Garden of Eden by Adam. This act of redemption through Jesus Christ would redeem mankind back to the right standard and fellowship with Jehovah God (Isaiah 7:14) & (Genesis 3:15). Their kingdom on the earth was ruled in defiance to God's laws by the spirit of Oppression and Depression, physically and or mentally to mankind.

The Assyrians culture began with Nimrod, yet the Assyrian people derived from **Asshur,** who was one of the most hideous and wicked figures of all history. He was cruel but a powerful soldier and a rugged Shepherd (Na. 3:18) and Jehu of Israel paid tribute to him.

I can see why God wanted the people of Nineveh to be saved so eagerly. All these people ever knew in life was wickedness. Look at who their leadership and founders were whose culture they had been following for years and years. (Jonah 4:10), they didn't even know their right hand from their left hand, **(Note* all they knew was evil.) What a compassionate God we serve.**

NIMROD THE BOUNTY HUNTER
Some paraphrase quotes from the Dake's Bible notes

---•❂•---

I began to research this **Nimrod.** I found out that the son of **Cush,** the son of **Ham,** the great grandson of **Noah** was this **Nimrod.** He began to be a mighty one in the earth. His name alone means we will **Rebel,** which points to some violent and open rebellion against **God.** He hunted down beast and man. His rebellion is associated with the beginning of his kingdom, and suggests that his hunting and mighty deeds were related primarily to hunting men by exercise of power. He oppressed them by rule and force, (**oppress** means to be pressed by heavy weight or burden by force). This was according to **Josephus, Flavius**, who was a Jewish historian born in Jerusalem, who along with other writers wrote the Tar gums.

Though not mentioned in the Bible he has contributed great revelation of scriptures **Nimrod** persuaded men not to assign their happiness to **Jehovah God,** because he declared to be their god. He became a great leader to build walls around cities for protection against the wild beasts and other animals. There were no walls around the city in those days. **Nimrod** lorded over the people, as most of the people gave tribute to him for his great strengths and concerns for their well being. Yet Nimrod was oppressing and hunting by destroying all who opposed him as being the sovereign god in their lives. He was a terror to the people.

Can you see the man running from Nimrod with all of his might to save his own life? Then a beast began to run aside of him, for fear of his life also? Yet he would hunt down the wild beast to protect the people, but he would also hunt down the man for not yielding to him, and making him supreme lord **of his life. I guess at this point the old saying, don't help me help the bear is applicable.**

As **Nimrod** and **Asshur** and other great warriors would build walls and cities, around the people, this would be the beginning of empires. It wasn't necessarily divine originations assuring law and order among men as ordained by **God** to **Noah.** In Genesis chapter nine, **Nimrod** deeds and achievements were not governed by obedient laws. He was a strong man and a giant renown for wickedness, a powerful warrior and king. He established one of the first wicked kingdoms on earth, and the first great universal false religion opposing **Jehovah God.** Along with the laws of God. This was done before the Lord with all defiance, yet being so opposing in the sight of **God** with his rule and power to build the tower of **Babel.** That is why God, Himself and the host of heaven came down to see **Babel,** and took action to counteract the rebellion of **Nimrod. (Genesis 10:5) (Literal Babylon is the site of the first great demon religions and idolatry in scripture).**

For surely this is indeed the first act of **Oppression** mentioned in the Bible. But then the question still comes to my mind. Why was this spirit of great rebellion in Noah's great grandson? The Lord showed me how this influence came about in the heavens when Satan rebelled against God and influenced **a third** of the angles to rebel with him (Revelation 12:4.) They were cast out of the heavens **into the earth**, where they had sex and married the natural women. They produced abnormal and wicked offspring. (Genesis 6:1-5) The offspring were giants, who **deceived the nations into destruction** along with their evil thoughts. It was lucifer, himself who influenced the king of Tyre and caused him to rebel against God (Ezekiel 28:1-2 and verse 13-19.) It was every rebellious spirit which had been cast into the earth from that point until now which operates in humans as well as animals, (Genesis 3:1-5) (Matthew 8:31-32.) Yet these opposing spirits which fell with satan operates in mankind today (Romans1:18-32.) It brings with them fear, <u>false evidence appearing real</u> (2Timothy 1:7), and this is one spirit that we know that God did not give us. Genesis 6:4 says that there were giants in the earth in those days and also after that, meaning **<u>after the flood of Noah as well.</u>**

It has been revealed to me by the Holy Spirit, through the scriptures, as well as other research, that Nimrod himself as well as Asshur and Jezebel have been influenced to co-labor with this spirit of oppression, depression and rebellion. These evil and rebellious spirits fell to the earth along with Lucifer, the head of all rebellion. For they have many common denominators, as the spirit of satan, their forefather. Wherein these spirits are an overpowering force which gives you a mental and physical shutdown. This is often associated with a feeling of <u>sorrow, (Matt.26:38), (Luke 22:45)</u> and agony that would later manifest itself into a diabolical act of oppression and depression. Its aim is to steal, kill and to destroy all that God has already fore ordained to exist to glorify Jehovah God. While using their diabolical schemes of fear to oppress, with their power to rule, we know that the future antichrist is called the Assyrian. They were and still are causing terror in the land of the living (Ezekiel 32:22-23.)

Now we have unveiled the spirit of **Oppression** and **Depression. Luke 12:2** tells us that there is nothing covered that shall not be revealed and nothing hidden that will not be known to his disciples. Therefore I submit to you the reader that **Asshur** himself is the spirit of Depression.

Depression means: dejection, <u>a mental state of dullness</u>, hollow, and abasement, a sinking of a surface. Whereas **Nimrod himself** represents the **spirit of oppression. Oppress means: <u>the act of weighing down</u>, to harass, to overpower, hardship, dullness of spirit, as you can see these two spirits work together as co-labors of evil in their kingdoms.**

Nimrod the great grandson of Noah, and Asshur, the grandson of Noah, all of their influence was negative and of terror. It was the Assyrians who founded the land of Chileans and brought it to ruins and exiled the 10 tribes of Judah to Babylon. For even then they were the enemy to God's people, trying to stop the original plan of God, which is to bring forth the Messiah to deliver His people from eternal death, (Genesis 3:15.) Because satan, who is the head of these acts has been defeated at Golgotha, the place of skull (John 19:30), Jesus Christ, the son of the living God said it is finished, = satan is defeated.

I present to you, the reader these words of (Micah 5:4-6) KJV
(This is an end time prophecy for a rhema word today)

The Prophet of the Lord

And they shall stand and feed in the strength of the Lord, in the majesty of the name of the Lord his God; and they shall abide; for now shall he be great unto the ends of the earth.

And this man shall be the peace, when the Assyrian shall come into our land; and when he shall tread in our palaces, and then shall we raise against him seven shepherds, and eight principal men.

And they shall waste the land of the Assyria with the sword, and the land of Nimrod in the entrances thereof; thus shall he deliver our land, and when he treads within our borders.

Our Land is
Our territory of Mental and physical areas
Our coast and property of which God has given us
Our space is our Mental and physical state of mind
&
Our Borders are our boundary
Our Borders are our perimeter
Our Borders are the limitation line for unwanted guest

Our Borders has four sides and they are as follows:
Our Ministry 2. Our family 3. Our health 4. Our finances
(These areas of our land is always under attack by the enemy)

Delores A. Allen

When the enemies of oppression and depression come on your land

Numbers 10:9 says and if you go to war in **your land** against the enemy that oppressed you, then you shall blow an alarm with the trumpets; and you shall be remembered before the Lord your God and you **shall be saved from your enemies.**

There will be an inner feeling or discernment to know that they are on your land. Therefore blow the alarm = something is wrong, the trumpet for calling the assembling of the congregation = warfare earnestly in the spirit! By pulling down strongholds and casting down imaginations (**in the mind**) we must bring into captivity every thought to the obedience of Christ, (2 Corinthians10: 4-6.) Because our weapons are spiritual, and mighty, remember to put on your whole armor (Ephesians 6:11-13).
Because they have trespassed on to your land.

"Keep them out of your house, which is on your land"

You must understand that inside of your house is where you really live, for humanity is a three part being. We are spirit, which possess a soul but we live in a body; (2 Thessalonians 5:23) & (Genesis 1:7) therefore our body houses our inner man which consist of our soul and spirit, which is the true person.

Our soul = the realm of self-consciousness. It is where the personality lies, and it houses our emotions, that which feels. (Mark 14:34) My soul is exceeding sorrowful unto death.

Our spirit= The spirit of man is the heart of man which is the core. The spirit is that which knows; the mind, the seat of the will, and the conscience. It is this part of man that God speaks to and through; it is this part that God searches. (Proverbs 20:27)The spirit of man is a candle of the Lord.

Our body= is the **house** of the soul and spirit, for this is where you really live. The real you live inside of your body; the real you is soul and spirit.
Present your bodies as a living sacrifice (Romans 12:1).

"Your house is <u>not</u>, and should never be their house"

Jesus taught in (Matt. 12:43-45) that when the unclean spirit is gone out of a man, he walk through dry places, seeking rest, and finds none. Then he said, I will return

into my **house** from where I came out; and when he is come, he finds it empty, swept, and garnished.

However do understand that when this unclean spirit of Oppression and Depression come into your spiritual house, it dramatize and terrorize the situation or circumstance at hand concerning one or more of your borders which are: Your faith (ministry) Your Family (love ones) Your Health (physical body) Your Finances (your livelihood)

Now Fill Your House

Fill the house with Faith in **the word of God**, and **the fruits of the Spirit**, the house must be filled in order to keep unwanted quest out. (Ephesians 6:10-16) & (Galatians 5:22)

Only Our Lord And Savior, Jesus Christ, Jehovah God And The Precious Holy Spirit Has Legal Authority To Cross Your Borders

Even though this scripture in Micah 5:4-6 is a prophecy of the future antichrist, know what the Lord is saying to us today. This same spirit of both the Assyrian and Nimrod will be allowed by tyranny spiritual force to operate as the spirits of . . .

<u>Oppression and Depression</u>

And when he comes into our land, and when he treads within our borders know that Jesus shall <u>stand and feed</u> in the strength of his God, Jehovah

The spirit of Oppression and Depression shall be defeated in this Dispensation and the dispensation to come

Even though **Jesus** was the living physical word of God, during the dispensation of the law, yet He is, and always will be the written word of God. **Acts 10:38** tells us, how God anointed **Jesus of Nazareth** with the Holy Spirit and with power, who went out doing good, **and healing all that were oppressed of the devil.** My grandmother, my mother, and uncle, as well as a host of relatives who has passed on to glory after experiencing the overpowering spirit of oppression and depression, did not understand the revelation of the power that Jesus has given to each of them to tread over scorpions and serpents and over all the power of the enemy (**Luke 10:19.**) We are healed today, according to the immutable word of God (**Hebrew 6:18.**) God can not lie, and His word provide healing, whether it takes place now or later (**Rev.21: 4.**) I do honor each one of my family members today, for each one of them has inspired me to hold on to my faith, and never give up, as they exemplified this to me on numerous occasions.

My Family Members Are Indeed A Great Cloud Of Witnesses

All passed away in faith, not having received the promises, but having seen them afar off, and were persuaded of them and embraced them, and confessed that they have a eternal life in Christ. Therefore I give eight stars of Honor to those as follows: eight stars represent a new beginning of eternal life in God (Numbers 24:17.) They are as follows:

Dedication And Honored In Memory
Eight Stars

Frances Deloris Atkins (My Mother)
Alice Pittman (Grand Mother)
Mary Warren (Great Grand Mother)
Thelma Freeman (Aunt)
Dorothy Parker (Cousin)
Gladys Powell (Aunt)
Ruth Clark (Aunt)
Alice Hunt (Aunt)

Honored in memory

Willie Pittman (Step-Grandfather)
Joe Atkins (Uncle)
Eddie B. Warren (Uncle)
Darnell Carney (Daddy)
Sherry Mclease (Cousin)
Mary Lezzy (Aunt)
Rosalee L. Boone (my best friend)

And to my family members who are still with us today that have not yet passed on to glory. My prayer is that every genetic generational curse of mental illness, be cut off in the bloodline, (Exodus 20:5-6) and that Jehovah God will continue to show mercy to those who love him, as we look to the hills which comes our strength, (Luke 22:43.)

My family, as well as **your** family, has the opportunity of possessing clarity and knowledge in God's written word for healing and deliverance of oppression and depression, according to their faith. Also any other mental illness as they walk in liberation whereby Christ has made us free, (Ephesians 4:8.) And as they journey on to their pre-ordained destiny in God, through Jesus Christ (Jeremiah 1:5) and (Jeremiah 29:11) because we do indeed have an expected end in God. Thus shall he deliver us from the Assyrian, <u>when he comes into our land, and when he treads within our borders (Micah 6:6.)</u>

Remember it starts in the spiritual realm
Before manifesting to the physical realm

Causes Of Diabolic Oppression and Depression

To Manifest To The Physical Realm

Biological, psychological, and social factors all play a role in causing depression. The diathesis-stress model in the brain, encounters this role in the depression. As a result of a pre-existing vulnerability, or diathesis, which <u>is a disposition toward or aptitude for a particular mental development and is activated by stressful life events.</u> The pre-existing vulnerability can be either <u>Genetic,</u> implying an interaction between Nature verses Nurture. This <u>is the inherent character or basic constitution of a person.</u> Psychology <u>is the mental or behavioral characteristics of an individual,</u> resulting from views and experiences in a person's life as well as their surroundings being observed in childhood and adulthood.

Genealogy

In cells, a gene is a portion of DNA, that contains both "coding" sequences that determine what the gene does, and "non-coding DNA" sequences that determine when the gene is active (gene expression). When a gene is active, the coding and non-coding sequences are copied in a process called transcription genetics, producing an RNA copy of the gene's information. This piece of RNA can then direct the synthesis of protein via the genetic code.

Normal Cohort of people

By researching and documenting over a period of time, it has shown how depression emerged among an initially normality statistics of people as well. Researchers concluded that variation among the serotonin transporter (5-HTT) gene affect the chances that people who have dealt with <u>very stressful life events will go on to experience depression.</u>

Antidepressants

Most antidepressants medications increase the levels of one or more of the monoamines—the neurotransmitters **serotonin**, **norepinephrine** and **dopamine**—in the chemical synapse between neurons in the brain. Some medications affect these monoamine receptors directly.

"Norepinephrine may be related to alertness and energy as well as anxiety, attention, and interest in life; [lack of] serotonin to anxiety, obsessions, and compulsions; and dopamine to attention, motivation, pleasure, and reward, as well as interest in life, The proponents of this theory recommend the choice of an antidepressant with mechanism of action that impacts the most prominent symptoms. Anxious and irritable patients should be treated with SSRIs or norepinephrine reuptake inhibitors, and those experiencing a loss of energy and enjoyment of life with norepinephrine—and dopamine-enhancing drugs,

1. Do take your medications
2. Do eat a well balance diet
3. Do exercise
4. Do meditate on the word of God. And allow your faith to manifest to the physical realm

"The Mind And The Brain Are Integrated"
Casting down imaginations, and every high thing that exalteth itself against the knowledge of God (2 Corinthians 10:5)

The brain monitors and regulates the body's actions and reactions. It continuously receives sensory information, and rapidly analyzes this data and then responds, controlling bodily actions and functions. **The brain stem** controls breathing, heart rate, and other autonomic (acting independently of volition—controlled by the nervous system process. **The NE cortex** is the center of higher-order (the mind) **thinking, learning,** and **memory.**

Post-traumatic stress disorder = There are several causes

Post-traumatic stress disorder (PTSD) is an anxiety disorder which results from a traumatic experience. It can result from long term (chronic) exposure to a severe stressor. Common symptoms includes avoidant behaviors, anxiety, anger and **depression.**

In my case, there was one traumatic episode after another, throughout my life, which had built up to manifest itself to the natural evidence. You must step out on faith, then take a leap of faith, and then allow your faith to take you on a journey. For in this journey of faith I do realize that in my praise and worship while yet still giving God the Glory that it takes me to a new level and dominion in Jesus Christ as I spiritually sat at His feet in heavenly places (Ephesians 2:5-6)

I am totally healed and delivered in my mind today without any medication, and because I am healed in my mind, I am also healed in my body.
I give God all the glory and the praise

(Isaiah 53:5)

For He sent his word and healed me

(Psalms 107:20)

Therefore I ask this question to you the reader

What Are **You** Going To Do

When They Come For **You?**

(The spirit of oppression and depression)

Amen